PILLOW TALKS WITH MY SOUL

by

René Wilmoth

authorHOUSE®

AuthorHouse™
1663 Liberty Drive
Bloomington, IN 47403
www.authorhouse.com
Phone: 1 (800) 839-8640

Published by AuthorHouse 11/19/2015

ISBN: 978-1-5049-1843-5 (sc)
ISBN: 978-1-5049-1844-2 (hc)
ISBN: 978-1-5049-1842-8 (e)

KJV

Scripture quotations marked KJV are from the Holy Bible,
King James Version (Authorized Version). First published in 1611.
Quoted from the KJV Classic Reference Bible,
Copyright © 1983 by The Zondervan Corporation.

Print information available on the last page.

Any people depicted in stock imagery provided by Thinkstock are models, and such images are being used for illustrative purposes only. Certain stock imagery © Thinkstock.

This book is printed on acid-free paper.

TABLE OF CONTENTS

Introduction/ About the book

Rene' reveals her most intimate thoughts in "Pillow talks with my soul." The book brings the topic of love and soul searching into a plain and intriguing light. Poem titles like 'God hates pedophiles', 'White Jesus, 'Love me' and 'Negros Like you' are among pieces that are written to get the reader thinking and leave poetry lovers entertained.

Pillow talks with my soul explores themes such as love, anger, depression, frustration, desire, internal conflict and peace. There are varying expressions that ranges from the playful " Love me like super models love diamonds in the poem 'Love Me' to hard core statements like "...negros like you deserve to die the way you did" from the poem 'Negros Like You.'

Pillow talks with my soul may evoke a smile, a nod or even a tear but it is sure to leave the reader thinking or left asking questions such as "I don't know where I have gone, can you find me?"

LOVE

GOD HATES PEDOPHILES

When I was a child, homosexuality was the greatest sin behind not paying tithes and offering, of course

But today, homosexuality has been promoted to various ranks of prestige (all even in churches)

And you know, they even have gay parades nowadays!

But you know who I hate? Pedophiles.

Yes, Pedophiles and I often wonder if God hates them too

And if I had a gun then I would have shot six shots into the perimeter of his left chest

And a seventh one for good measure

Garnish

And I did

So why is it that it is my heart that is bleeding and why am I the one drowning in this sea of unforgiven blood?

Cold sweat blistering like cold sores in my soul

Does God hate Pedophiles?

The only sinners incapable of repentance and the only sinners incapable of forgiveness!

And a voice whispers to me, "Let him without sin cast the first stone."

"Hush no tell nobody or else mi kill yuh!"

"Gas dem and light dem!"

He was 9 when it first started and she was 13 when it first happened

And that beast was 5 when they first did it to him

That is when they first touched him and he vowed to become the monster he now is but nobody would ever listen to him now

Not. Even. God.

And none will get close enough to hear his side of the story

But this is an open and shut case, no pun intended

So in an open letter to God he writes:

"I am sorry but I can't promise that I won't do it again because of this thing.

That thing that keeps pulling me like an electromagnetic force of eternal damnation!"

"Can you help me?"

But I know that God did not answer back because He hates Pedophiles!

Like seriously, they hurt children

There is no way that God can love pedophiles?

And I write a letter to God and in it I write:

"Why am I still holding my stone?"

René Wilmoth

LOVE LETTER

You are the most awesome lover that I have ever known

How can your love be so pure and flawless even in the sight of jealousy?

How can your love penetrate the darkest depths of my heart?

How can you continue to love me when I fail to love your children?

You continue to be faithful to our relationship and continually shower me with your love even when my heart is with another!

You do not consume me with your jealousy

You continue to bring me chocolate and roses even when I am reluctant to return your love, your calls!

You stand by daily and watch me cheat with another yet you will always be there when I finally come home

My awesome lover

My immaculate friend

My precious one

Gold and diamonds are not even a fraction of your splendor and beauty

Your love is a like a flawless creature

The truth of your affection is like a summer sunset

Your aroma is like that of freshly cut flowers

Your smile is that of a whisk of cool winter breeze in midsummer

Your touch like that of a clean bird's feather

Your love is so boundless that it saturates every atom in my anatomy

You love me for who I am

My selfish and multi-flawed self

You love me when I do something nice to impress you

You love me when I am stumbling and embarrassed

You love me when I am clean and cuddly and just as much when I am dirty too

Your personality is that of a protective father

Your presence that of the Supreme Being

You, I will trust to love me forever, my perfect and compassionate Lover

I will always love you

René Wilmoth

TEN REASONS TO LOVE ME

I love your beautiful smile and the way your whole face glow when you do

I love the gentle arches of your waist and how they reach for your hips

I adore the way you make beautiful sandwiches and align them on my plate

I am fascinated by the way you pause when you speak as though to allow the words to caress my mind as they flow to my soul

I love the way the mole on your lip reminds me of the place you hold in my heart; a small permanent space

I love the way you evoke words and coerce them to dance to your tune

I love the way you laugh and the way you make me laugh

I love your energy, your charisma and charm

I love your white eyes, your smooth skin and beautiful fingernails

I love your body, soul and spirit because of the way they warm mine

LOVE ME

Love me like I deserve it

Love me like you care

Love me like you never did yesterday

Love me like there is no tomorrow

Love me like super models love diamonds

Love me like politicians love lies

Love me like prisoners love freedom

Love me like little girls love dolls

Love me like little boys love mischief

Love me like flies love light

Love me

René Wilmoth

Love me like you mean it

Love me when I am listening

Love me when I am paying attention

Love me 'til the galaxy applauds the sacred bond we share

Love me when ointments have taken the place of my perfume

Love me when loose dentures slide from my lips when I sleep

Love me when the exotic whispers that we shared have become sweet memories we have grown too old to remember

Love me till our wedding bands metamorphosis into white gold particles deeply etched into our souls!

Love me!

TOMORROW

Tomorrow is a big day

A day that will signal the beginning of your life and mine

The beginning of a new life for us

Of the freeing of our souls from sure doom

Not a magical but a miraculous day

When I will start to forgive you as you forgive me

A day to start anew

Tomorrow is symbolic of the most glorious day in human history

Tomorrow is the beginning of the day that I will start to love you again

Tomorrow is why I have the strength to get through today

Tomorrow is why I came to visit

Tomorrow is why I bought you presents

René Wilmoth

Tomorrow is the reason you deserve it

Tomorrow is why we are all here

Tomorrow is not yet here but in advance I say

"Merry Christmas, my darling"

Anger/ Depression

NOT NOW! I'M ANGRY!

It has gotten to the point where it is not about controlling my anger anymore but about completely getting rid of the monster inside of me that causes my blood to boil

It's about not silencing but terminating the vibrations in my nervous system and that slight increase in my blood temperature

I will tell you what happens to control it

When I get so angry that I want to shout and scream and break a hundred glass

But I can't because I am at work

So instead

I stiffen my neck, speed down the corridor and feel my blood warm up in my veins

And for the next few hours I won't be able to concentrate and won't care either

No one that I know will be able to console me, I don't regard them enough

I always feel justified when I'm angry

I am always right

Always have a right to lose control, behave boisterously- Ghetto even

Or keep talking loudly and speedily to keep up with the rate of my heart beat

Just to ensure that everyone in the vicinity gets my point and hears my voice, "dem niggers done barked up the wrong tree"

I would just shout long enough to let them know that they dare not talk to me like that

Then I realize that learning to control my anger was not going to be enough

This is because sometimes I do

Even so, I would still need time to blow off some steam

There are other times when I can't

The times when anger has its own agenda and will not listen to me at all

It always has just one more point to prove, always justified

Then I learnt not to just control anger but get rid of anger and started seeing some changes

I will only own the things that God has given me through education, training, family and friends

I will work to eradicate the pest of the good social fabric of my life - this thing called anger

I want to get to the point where someone can say something totally wrong and my blood not only warm up and cool down in my vein

But that I will be able to smile, sincerely

It is ok to be angry if we do not sin

I, being human will make mistakes

I just don't want to be a time bomb waiting to go off

I don't want any readymade 'up' inside me just waiting to be 'set'

I want a peace from the inside

There is no justification for losing control and continuing to lose control

I must rid myself of this 'crosses'

I must move beyond allowing some petty distorted emotion to control my life

I will not let anger destroy the profound and good things that awaits in the horizon

Neither will I let it rob me of wonderful opportunities

I will not let anything control me!

DEPRESSED BEYOND RECOGNITION

I feel like a scandal bag being blown aimlessly down a deserted street

I feel an intense combination of depression, anger, hate and defeat

I have never felt so used, abandoned and unloved

I would never have envisioned that the very sight of people from my past could bring me to tears

I thought I knew better than to feel like useless "unrecyclable trash"

I thought I knew better than to feel broken, splintered and lost

I thought I knew better than to give up

I thought I knew better than to cry night after night over the same thing

I thought I knew better than to depend so much on external love,

the love that I have for myself should have kept me

I thought I knew better than to feel that if even

one person loved me for me;

Not the epitome of the success that I was,

or the prospect of the greatness that I can achieve

Love me for me

the me whose living expenses exceed my earnings,

the me who is emotionally a junk yard,

the me who does not have much to offer emotionally or otherwise

the me who is broken and weary

Will you love me please?

Anyone

Strong Woman

Strong women don't cry

They are hard and strong

Immune to all emotional trauma

Brave, courageous and charismatic

Has this tragedy weakened my character, joy peace or my happiness?

Can an alien survive in the real world?

How can you live with someone all your life and not know them?

Why didn't I spend time to get to know myself?

I am no super hero

I have challenges to face like everyone else

I do not trust myself, there is still some secret between us

I keep finding out new things everyday

What will I find out tomorrow?

I cry like a baby

I do stupid things

I am childish at times

I am immature impulsive and weak!

Who taught you to believe this nonsense?

You are not stupid

You are not weak

Do not give up!

Even Jesus wept!

Who said that you are stupid they thought John the Baptist was mad!

Who said that you are childish, 'Lest you become as little children you cannot see God!'

Who said that it is wrong to cry?

'Tears are a language that God understands!'

René Wilmoth

Weeping man

Tears have become a permanent feature of his living young tearful corpse

They have taken permanent residence in the pores of his face

They have eliminated his smile

They have created a stream in his tear glands, so full of hate, so full of anger, so full of fear

I can't recall seeing his face without those tearstained cheeks and those cold sad eyes

The light in his eyes no longer linger but only flicker and go out

I pray for the day when a real smile would linger on his face

When those tear marks would linger and die

When that infinite fountain of tears would dry up and vanish

I pray for the day his smile returns

But for now, my hands will toil day and night to wipe his tears

Circus clown mode to make him want to live again

I will wear my achievements like a crown to let him see that he too can achieve and even much more than I

I want to teach him to walk like a king

Like he has the power to create miracles with his mind

Like he can still be a man even though he often cry

I will teach him that his tears can be used as a shipping dock to get him to his destination in life

I will be the umbrella that he needs in the rain

I will show him that he is not alone

Never alone with me here

Tell him that his sister will always have his back!

January First

God?

Yes, down here in the bathroom

I know that this is a New Year celebration and everyone is outside laughing and having fun and I can hardly concentrate above the loud noise and excitement

I don't want to sound like a hypocrite or anything (but I know you would want me to put the best face out and smile, right?)

Anyway, it was required of me to be at this party tonight and the news of it made me nervous since I knew I would need a massive facial and hairdo and my Christmas bonus was not even enough!

But I made the sacrifice to look beautiful tonight

I took a few hundred dollars and bought a bright and genuine smile from an old lady

Forgive me, but I had been so unhappy most of last year and so every time I squeezed a smile it just wouldn't come out right!

I kind of stole the forehead of a new born baby since mine had grown wrinkled from all the snorting and frowning (It's not my fault Lord, you know how terrible my boss is and the people around me!)

I have developed major dental problems because of cussing and swearing (but what would you expect from someone you allow to have so many problems)

And this I must complain took days of preparation and search to find since even among the Christians I found it difficult to find a suitable pair of dentures, gladly I got these to borrow from a young lady

I stayed up many nights on my back thinking of how wicked people can be and how I cannot even afford a luxurious life

As a result, my eyes have developed bags under them

My face is slightly tear stained and the back of my hair is partially gone

I honestly thought I was not going to make it to this party tonight

The Christians have spent many nights crying for themselves, their families and even strangers too

The college and university students have also spent many night between studying and partying

And many workers in this country have spent days and nights working late and worrying about their children

And I could go on…..

It seem it would take me until after the new year to find such a face so I kind of just went to the nearest beauty salon and applied eye shadow, mascara, blush and sort of cut the back of my hair into the newest new year hair style

I lost a lot of weight but as least slim is in and this dress looks gorgeous on me (might I say so myself)!

God, I don't mean to sound miserable or anything and thank you for providing the money so that I could cover my shame

But Lord, it has not even been two hours into the party and my makeup has already faded

My smile is fake again

And my gut even looks bloated from eating all that junk!

I can't help but to think how badly I am going to feel when I wake up tomorrow

I am still very unhappy

I still have my problems

And honestly

New Year for me is just another sad day with millions of people worldwide pretending to be happy!

Who, by the way, will be at least a few hundred dollars poorer by the next day!

Truth is Lord, I don't have any New Year's resolution

I don't have any sense of direction

I hardly have any true friends

And I am not even sure why we are celebrating the New Year

Is it to wake up to another day of sorrow and pain?

I am locked in the bathroom sitting on the floor crying my heart out

And everyone is outside drinking and cheering on the New Year

When I go back out there

I will be as happy as everyone else

But right now, I have to be honest

I know that I am not the nicest cookie in the jar

I have done some shameful things

But I want you to change me

Can you?

Will you?

Please help me to change my ways and walk with me this year!

There is so much that I do not understand

Please teach me

When I leave this party and go home

I am going to be lonely

But please come with me

Thank you for listening

I feel better already!

Crumble

If you find yourself crumbled into a pitiful mass at the foot of your bed for whatever reason, small or great

If you find yourself yearning to get as close as possible to the floor just so that your body can physically match the 'lowness' that you feel in your soul

If tears come rushing down your face despite your efforts to tame them; the source of your breakdown first time or recurrent

Know that you are not the first to be crumbled into this fetal like position slapping your head while repeating

Stupid

Stupid

Stupid

If you find yourself clutching your chest in a desperate effort to compress your pain

Whether it was something SHE said

Or something HE did

Or something you wish YOU never did

Remember that it happens to all of us

And the rest of us too!

You will smile again after the floor no longer bears evidence of your mini-breakdown

You will live to cry again

Hours after this saga will find you laughing out loud

There is no shame in this moment

No shame in tear-ING

You will surely heal

And become stronger

Pick yourself up and stand tall again!

Frustration

TIRED

My knees have grown tired from descending my ego like a lonely staircase to get to you

So, if tomorrow I lose the will to be devoted to you

Remember that today I cared for you more than I ever did anyone else

Remember that today I built monuments to the fact that I exhaled the essence of your charm

Remember that I redecorated my bedroom with tears because of you

Remember that I broke all my rules for you every single time

Remember that I use to love kissing you under the mango tree

Remember that I will never regret taking comfort in your presence

Remember that I took the chance give a stranger the key to my heart

Remember me, the girl you flirted with but chose not to love!

René Wilmoth

I WILL SURVIVE

I am so weak Lord

I have so little energy

But today I will write

Today I will record my troubles

Today will fight through the invisible odds against me

Today I will ignore my growling stomach

Today I will let my clothes stretch as they will

Today I will ignore my broken slipper strap

Today I will not drown in self pity

Today I will remain proud

Today I will not hang my head in shame

Today I am still waiting for deliverance

Lord I am here waiting on you, today.

CONTENTMENT

Did I ever ask you to let the poverty go away?

Did I ever desire to have my problems elope with the wind?

Did I ever complain about the potholes in my road?

Did I ever complain of not having enough to wear?

Did I ever complain of not being able to spend weekends in fancy hotels?

Did I ever complain about the friends that you gave me?

Did I ever say that they are not worthwhile?

Did I ever complain about my Jordan that when I cross it I will have to wash the mud off

Well, I just want to say sorry

Sorry that I ever complained because without problems I could not survive

There was a time when I barely had enough

A time when I went to bed with hardly enough in my stomach and no idea of what I would have to eat the following day

I can remember scraping through the rubble, as it were, just to find enough

Yet you were there Lord and I was happy

Happy when I had to watch the fruit trees outside my windows and just hoping that the fruits will be ready in time for the next meal or laughing at the fact that I have acquired the taste for food I would have otherwise deemed 'despicable'

Would spend more time in prayer talking to you, asking questions and hoping that you would tell me what I want to hear and even when I did not hear you answer, I would still speak to you

On the contrary Lord, now that I have a little more I am utterly miserable and can't stop thinking about the things that I want so badly and still can't seem to have

I went shopping today and yet there is so much that I still don't have

I came home miserable because of all the bills and perils ahead

I feel so miserable

The cupboard is full but I still can't find what I want to eat

Lord, I just feel so miserable

Please help me

DREADFUL CERAMIC

I have seen floors before, but this here ceramic is the most dreadful of them all

This here floor seemed to have been tie and dyed with black, gray and silver with orange nail polish splashed over it

This here floor produces baby centipedes, millipedes and bugs!

This here floor is not overtly cold like the others before but it is the coldest that I have been in such intimate contact with

This here floor is so smooth that the smoothness is evident through the thin veneers of fabric that separates us

This here floor,

Hopefully my temporary dwelling place

I thought we would have been travelling separate roads by now but our parting has been postponed until

So if this is the way it is going to be then let's take care of each other until fate bids us farewell

This here ceramic

My temporary dwelling place

René Wilmoth

11 months then, now I'm almost 22

I can't remember crying after you then but I must have didn't I?

How many times did I crave your touch?

How many nights did I go to sleep with you on my mind knowing that you will not be there when I woke up?

How many times were you there to wipe my nose?

How often were you there to dry my tears?

To listen to my childish bickering; to laugh at my stale jokes,

To slap my face when I was rude, to lift me when I fell?

Where were you when I silently suffered abuse and rejection?

Where were you when I collected my trophies?

Where were you when I needed you?

What is your role?

For what purpose are you so called?

I feel lonely and lost but I expect you to be there for me

I have waited for over two decades for you to return with my favourite cereal, juice and a doll maybe

But in vain I have waited for you to rescue me

The sky has darkened the stars are bright and still I can't see your face

I wonder if you love me

Do you even know the meaning of love?

Do you even know how to show it?

Why didn't you come back?

Why did you leave me in the first place?

Was I not precious enough?

Or was I going to prevent you from having fun or 'living your life'

I thought I had forgiven you

I thought things would be different now

I thought that you changed

I woke up the other day in a panic

I thought I had everything figured out but I was wrong

I was frantic; I desperately needed someone to talk to

Eureka! I thought I could just give you a call and we could talk

But my fingers froze before I started dialing

Face reality I told myself

What would she know and besides I would have to start from the beginning after all it would be like calling a complete stranger

So, I didn't

What would I say to her or what could she tell me

So tonight I will sit here and pray that she will return to me tomorrow with a doll and stay with me this time

I hope she will return someday in mind, body and spirit

I don't play with dolls anymore I reminded myself!

Ah well

Whatever

Desire

OUT OF REACH

I cannot deny the power of love because it existed long before I

And will remain long after my last chapter ends

But I must admit that I love love

The idea of love and everything in between

But shall I spend my short life searching after it

Shall I yearn for its light to find my path

Shall I chase this thing 'clearly' too good for me

Shall I chase it till I die

Shall I waste my life yearning or shall I continue to pretend that I do not want to be loved

Or shall I chase like fools do or be chased

Or stay single until I'm dead

Why do I care to be loved?

Is love the source of life?

I have nourishment and oxygen and a few other things

Shall I care that men are the most interesting of things God created

Must I admit that a good man is rare commodity?

A commodity, I guess, I cannot afford

Must I say that I fear I will never find a man

Must I say that I love their eyes

Must I say that I sometime stare

Must I admit that I am like other fools

Must I say that I know it is a beautiful thing

Must I say that I will die without if I must

I cannot condemn love but I will deny it if I must

This may be a passing thought or a reckless emotion

But the power of real love cannot be defined by passing thoughts or confined to reckless emotions

KRYPTONITE

I do not trust this flesh of mine

This flesh of mine is causing me

To stumble

And fumble

And grumble

I am at the entrance of sexual sin's door

for my flesh it magnifies my loneliness much more than before

He wants sex

I want love and comfort,

A fair exchange to me

I know you'll disagree

If only I had not loved you Jesus

If only I had not promised to be faithful to you

then I swear I would have fallen

I would have given him anything

Anything to make him love me,

Anything to make him care,

I wanted nothing more than to make him my closest friend

But thanks to you, I am no fool

My flesh has caused my heart to be saturated with pain

My flesh, my kryptonite

I THINK

I think your younger son is cute

I think I am in love with your older son

He's in love with someone else!

But if I ever have a mother- in –law

I'd want her to have your eyes

I'd want her to smile at me the way you do

I'd want her to kiss me like you do

If I ever have a mother-in-law, I would want her to love like you
do- with your everything

René Wilmoth

If I ever have a mother- in-law

I'd want her to be you!

But that can't ever be true

So, when I pray the next time that I do

I will ask God to send me one just like you!

Internal Conflict

WHITE JESUS

If there is any power left in You

If there is a God – then reach down your hand and touch my pain
in that place that cannot be reached by any other

In that empty nest called my heart

In that place that cannot be reached by my tears

That cannot be comforted or saturated with kind words

That can no longer see you

That no longer notices when the stars stand in ovation and
acknowledge you as the great I am

That no longer wakes to the kiss of your Holy Spirit

That no longer esteems you above all other gods

That no longer talks to you

That no longer trusts you

White Jesus or whatever colour you are!

Can you hear me?

Can you feel my pain?

Can you love a nobody who nuh come from no weh?

Can you love a person so lost I cannot even find myself?

Can you love a person who ingests insanity and excretes profanity?

Can your blood wash a person who knows the Word from cover to cover yet refuses to believe a word?

White Jesus or whatever colour you are . . .

I don't know where I have gone

Can you find me?

FOR DADDY'S GIRLS

He doesn't care about me, does he?

I promise I won't let him use me!

Dad, I know that he may end up walking on my heart like a carpet on his way to another woman's heart

But right now it's going to hurt so much to let him go

Even though I know this my heart bleeds from the inside

Can I desire him for just five more minutes?

If I have to choose between the two of you, You know that I will choose You

But why do I have to choose anyway?

Can't you talk to him?

You are an established man

You have all the links

You can change him!

If you don't want to answer me now I will get upset and go lock myself in my room

Dad, before I do, can I curl up in your arms and weep for a while?

Since I am not allowed to cry myself to sleep in his arms

May I cry myself to sleep in Yours?

And Dad when I fall asleep could you tuck me in bed and cover me with my yellow blanket

Please lock the door when you leave

Dad, I don't always understand you but I love you

Dad, am I still Your little angel?

PATIENT NO. 1 MILLION 32

This baby has been driving on empty for a year now

This baby feels like checking into a hospital that deals with people with my kind of pain

The three fold kind of pain that's generously garnished with confusion and despair

I hope this one is benign

I hope there are antibiotics for it

I hope the symptoms won't last

We put our trust in people and things that inevitably fail us

We laugh and cry bitter sweet tears and cuddle and make fake memories

We dance vainly to music we don't appreciate and smile all the way through our open heart surgeries

We let our engines run too long and often on empty and suffer too long in strange places

We laugh and dance with our bodies while our souls are being dragged away in shackles kicking and screaming by the enemy

Our bodies eventually begin to collapse under the pressure, the nutrition is weak, the heart begins to palpitate and the knees buckle

Somebody call a taxi. I need to go to the hospital, somebody please

I need to lie flat on my back

I am going to check myself into a hospital

I need to lie flat on my back

My knees have refused to support me

I can't take this life anymore

My heart can't take this anymore

Somebody call this number

Nurse, call this number

A short brown lady with a sweet voice is going to be on the other end of the line

Please tell her that her granddaughter needs her to come get her

Somebody please call my grandma!

Peace/Gratitude

HIDEAWAY

I have gone to a place where you cannot find me

No one shouts at me here

No one screams my name

Here all my bills are paid

Here, I only wear what makes me feel comfortable

Here, I walk and play in tall grass that do not itch

Sometimes I stop to have a drink - of water

But if you ever find me here

I hope you are good company

And I hope you say my name out loud

And I hope you enjoy the simple pleasures of life that I do

I really hope that you find me

Live in the moment

I often spent most of my todays planning for a better tomorrow

Better grades, the dream house, the dream partner, the dream child, a better job, a better education, to be in better shape, the more polished look, the cloudless days, the 'mareless'nights

Graduating from anger management!

Too little time to appreciate today, to enjoy God's presence in this small space in this small corner while I sleep here on this cold floor!

Too busy thinking of a mansion to enjoy the coziness of my one bedroom

Too busy thinking of fast food to enjoy 'turn cornmeal'

Too busy thinking of a mansion to enjoy the comfort of a one bedroom

Too busy thinking about pillow tops to enjoy the subtle comfort of foam

Too busy thinking of the ideal partner to bother to understand the ones who are for real

Those who really care

Too busy trying to achieve more to applaud ourselves for having reached thus far

Too busy thinking about the things that we do not have to enjoy the things that we do have!

Smile even when you feel no need to

Smile and embarrass your pain

Smile until it becomes a part of you

Live in the moment

Failure

FAILURE'S SHADOW

Sometimes failure seems inevitable

Sometimes we simply fail to try

Sometimes we try hard at a particular task yet our efforts prove futile

We are often able to overcome tangible obstacles in life such as tying our laces and making the bed

Yet we often stumble upon the laces of intangible obstacles such as lack of persistence and endurance

I guess if we do not experience the bitter taste of defeat, we cannot lavish in the glory of being successful

Life is a giant maze in which we often feel trapped, subordinate to the superior gait of its 'unpredictabilities'

In my eyes, success is always out there though often hidden in the dark shadow of failure

Just look beyond failure, regret and remorse: true success is always out there if you persevere

René Wilmoth

TRY HARDER - NEVER STOP

I once allowed failure to motivate me to fail

When I failed at any task I would feel a sense of hopelessness

The more I failed, the more failure followed

I got to the point where I started to fail at the things that I was good at!

I felt lost and simply stopped trying which made things worse

I knew that something was seriously wrong with me so I told my fear to a man called Mr. J

Mr. J gave me a bottle labelled patience

He sent me to a magic well named perseverance

I was instructed to tie the bottle to a string of faith and use it to draw a liquid called Try Harder-Never Stop from the well and use it at every single task

So I tried Try Harder-Never Stop

I used it especially at the tasks that I think were most difficult

From then on, whenever I feel like allowing myself to fail simply because I stopped trying,

I would open the red closet called my heart, take out my little bottle of Try Harder- Never Stop and experience miracles.

Secrets Thoughts

I am Not Africa

Why do black people have different hair from all people?

Which part of Africa are you from?

Another is disappointed that a black girl like me could not tell where he was from by looking at the tribal marks in his face

You need to know your history!

I asked him if he knew the history of Jamaica

There was silence

How come a child is formed from 23 chromosomes from each parent; yet if mixed with black that child is 46 chromosomes black?

How come all black people are from Africa including the ones who have never been there and does not know the language?

And, if all black people are from Africa, where are all white people from?

You see them everywhere!

What do people mean when they ask, 'where are you from?'

And why does it even matter?

Who designs the labels created to box people in, make them feel small?

Only as big as our retinas will allow us to see them!

 I see colour

Never colour blind

Shades of colours that fills in our skin

I see colour

All beautiful shades of colour

Skin colours as diverse as the electromagnetic spectrum of light

But my thoughts are colourless and so is my soul

And if they were coloured somehow I do not think that it would matter

My black skin does not make me 'Africa" and neither does it make me 'Jamaica'

It means I am human with the ability to love any person despite the place that they hold in the box of crayon!

I am not 'Africa' and neither am I 'Jamaica'

I believe in a God who made all races and decided in which
country we should be born

And to which tune our ancestors danced

We are all from the same race

The human race!

Merely shaded in with different crayons

Made to love each other

But if you insist on giving me a label

I would rather you call me Christ-like!

Why I fell in love with Jesus

Why is it easier to say that you believe in "the universe"

Yourself as your own god

Or even a god created in your own mind

Not sure which god you serve, yet deny the one who exists in the very air you breathe

I open my mouth to speak the name of Jesus, there is a gentle reminder in my soul that one day I may be killed for the sake of this Christ I chose against all odds,

And a part of me cringes

And an even bigger part of me is prepared to return the favour He did for me by being hung on a tree

And I think of people who die each day for no apparent cause and those who live for no cause

As though their gods have guaranteed them some kind of tomorrow

As if their happiness is only confined to earthly "happy endings"

Or substances that pass through the alimentary canal

And I question why I decided to love this scorned Jesus

This Jesus dubbed "the white man's God!"

Yet is seem so few white men serve him!

How pitiful this God who made heaven, earth and us

Not impressive enough to be given a second look!

Not cool enough for pillow talks

Made flesh to dwell among us?

Laughable

Forget Him!

Let us serve ourselves and give in to our own desires

Let us cross Him out of our minds, wipe Him from our laws!

Let us be our own heroes

We will save ourselves

Let us forget the cross He rode like a chariot to bring our souls to victory and light!

I know my Jesus will not impress you

You have "seen and read too much"

To hell with this 'white man's religion'

His ways too simple

Jesus, lover of prostitutes, gays, cheaters, pimps, child molesters and all of us

Lover of blacks, whites and all of us

Jesus can be the cup of coffee we need to get us through our days

But you would rather bear the burden of your own soul and be your own god,

But I,

A cowardly sinner holds on to the cross like a designer clutch

Like my life depends on it

It does

I like the feel of this Jesus in my soul

The feel of His praises in my mouth

Oh how I love to shout

Thank you Jesus

My Perfect God!

And I know some will not love me for it!

Tributes to live people

My girlfriends, my heroes

They say women can be such…(you know)

Hating each other simply 'cause someone turned up to the party in a better weave than we did

And sometimes we look at another woman and

Just

Don't

Like them

But not my girlfriends,

My girlfriends are my heroes!

Beautiful women

Super model look alike chicks!

Loving my curves for days chicks

Asian chicks

Indian chicks

René Wilmoth

European chicks

African chicks

Caribbean chicks

American chicks

All kinds of chicks

Different chicks- same chicks

All fun to be with chicks!

Beautiful women from all over the world!

How dem pretty so?

They hold my hands

They teach me to breathe again

They teach me to walk again

Another jokes,

You are a fool!

They tell me I am beautiful

They say, you go girl!

We love you

You can do it

You going to be a star!

And I find strength in leaning on their shoulders

I feel warmth in their smiles

I feel love in their embrace

My girlfriends, my heroes!

René Wilmoth

Natural Beauty

Golden hair like rays of sunshine

Eyes as blue as the ocean

Lips like roses

Skin like delicate pink petals

Voice as calm as the wind

Blonde beauty, why do they call you plastic?

Porcelain Barbie doll look-alike beauty

Does that make you plastic?

Never associated with natural

No inner beauty

Only pure plastic

Does plastic bleed?

Does it cry itself to sleep at night?

Does it tell its story on the back of another woman's mistake?

Does it have to wear high heels just so it can be seen?

Blonde beauty- not blonde enough

Bleached blonde –too plastic

Do you ever feel?

Do you ever love?

Do you get tired of the labels?

Do they ever see pass your lipstick and blush?

Do they see pass your foundation, below your mascara and into your fear?

Do they stare pass your pain?

Do they ever desire to know your real name?

Blonde beauty- mere plastic?

Natural

Stunning

Blonde

Beauty!

The one that got away!

Women always speak of the men who treat them a little less that they deserve

But we do not often speak of the good ones that we made get away!

Mr. Right for us

Mr. Too Good To Be True, what do you want for me?!

The one who loved you so much that you keep looking behind you to see if he is really talking to you!

What did you just say?

You love me?

Those three words said way before your back was broad enough to carry them!

The one you broke up with because you were 'not sure' until he decided to leave

But I love you now!

Too late

I'm married to another woman

She is having my baby!

You are the only man I ever thought of as being perfect!

You were, right for me

I remember your face

I always wondered why it glowed

Your laughter

Your gentleness

Your charm

How you spoiled me rotten!

Mr. Nice Guy

You were always nice

I hope that she is good to you

I love you

Too late

I cannot leave her

But…

Too late

When the passion I feel for you have faded with the years

And the impression your smile created in my mind is replaced by another's

When old age has marinated in our bones and the children that you have with her are all grown

I will forever remember you as 'the one that got away!'

Other Poems

NEGROS LIKE YOU

If they asked somebody they would say that negros like you
deserve to die the way you did

Shot down in the street

Your dying body dragged away by unknown assailants

I picture them muffling your final gasps for breath while you bleed
to death

Gun shots ringing in my ears like a phone call years earlier:

Hello?!

Five year prison sentence, for what?

Gun charges

Phone call:

Hello?!

He's out of prison but can't get a job

They told the boss he has been to prison

Phone call:

Hello?!

He threatened to kill your mother

Phone call:

Hello?!

Hello. It's me. Don't believe anything they tell you

I never threatened to kill your mother

There was so much urgency in his voice

And somehow I knew they would kill him but still not prepared for this phone call:

They killed him

But gunmen

Not the police

It was only a matter of who would get him first

But my mind takes me to his last phone call to me

How I heard him pleading with me between the lines to forgive him

How he waited on the lines in silence to feel if I still loved him

I said something like, okay

And he may have heard the love in my voice

He hung up the phone quickly

He was never into the habit of staying long on the line

It is now too late for me to tell him that it is God who he needs to seek forgiveness from

Haunted by our last conversation I wonder if he figured that out even seconds before he joined the statistics of

Negro: Shot and killed by another negro!

WHO IS HE?

To them he may have been another mentally ill patient, the madman or just another vagrant

But to me he was a poor sad child, another broken spirit. Yet another soul that I failed to rescue

I should have spoken to him; I wish I could have held him in my arms for but a while

I wish I were able to make him smile

I wish my voice were able to soothe his pain

There was nothing between us but cheerful air particles, yet it appeared as though there was an invisible invincible glass that separated our bodies and souls

My soul sank in guilt as he chuckled and fidgeted like an innocent child

He threw the bag on the table like a child would, not enough to destroy it to but enough to express his anger

I watched him as though I knew him forever

I cared but did not show it

I wish I had another chance

Seeing him leave gave me a nostalgic feeling as I reflected on
the times that I had allowed vagrants, family and friends to leave
without saying I care, I love you or goodbye

René Wilmoth

WISE OLD WOMAN

A wise old woman once told me that I should never get so caught up in myself or achievements that I forget the people around me

So caught up with my new status, Mrs. Somebody that I forget to take time to pray

So caught up with trying to acquire wealth that I don't take time to give of the things that I already have

So caught up with the big things in my life that I forget to appreciate the little things and the little people

So busy using the power within that I forget the Person with all the power

Spend all my love on myself and therefore have none to give to others

Spend so much time trying to make myself happy that I worked myself into misery

Spend so much time talking about the things that I need to accomplish that I never find time to actually do them

Spend so much time worrying about the things that I didn't do to realize that I still have time to do the few that can still be done

GROWTH

It is always good to grow

Growth is special

Growth is symbolic of an unconscious achievement

This happens whether or not we deserve that achievement

Although chronological growth occurs spontaneously, it is not always preceded by mental maturity

I hope that in all your achievement and growth that you will not only grow older

In age I mean

But that you will grow to love and appreciate even more the small details and beauty that so magnificently encompass our fragile minds

The annoying cats

René Wilmoth

The soft lizards

The wind's soft kiss and mine

And the innocent souls that you meet in life, 'While you are on the road'

GRANDMA'S DREAM

How can you not love a woman who has dedicated her entire life to loving you?

A woman whose only dream was to make yours a reality,

A woman who never once complained about her dreams being unfulfilled as a result of her efforts to make you comfortable,

She scrubbed, ironed, baked, cooked, attended school functions, and endured lack just to ensure our happiness.

I wonder if her dream as a little child was to become the perfect mother to children she never gave birth to,

Her hobby; taking care of people's kids while they remain busy wasting their lives and never returning to pick them up as promised.

Did she not have any party to attend or men to flirt with?

For the only party that I knew her to attend were the ones held at church

Parties to which she brought us to, "dressed like puss foot"

Clothes for which she raised chicken, pigs and goats to afford

Indeed, she is a virtuous woman who laboured hard for her children, their children and other people's children too.

My grandma, a woman that I will always love

And who has always loved me

Grandma, I will always love you

PLAYER

Truth is, there was I time that I thought about you more than I did the average person

Truth is, there is something about being in your company that made me feel like hundreds of fireflies were dancing on my heart

Truth is, there was a part of me that has always told me that the sting of your rejection would temporarily cripple me

Mr. Hot Shot, you wore your good looks like a crown as though you had anything to do with the fact that God chose to make you beautiful

You in fact did nothing to deserve the good looks given to you.

So you thought I was one of those girls who you could wrap around your little finger, Mr. Hot shot

You in fact chose to 'bark up the wrong tree.'

You think that you are a player?

Consider yourself played by one who you thought knew nothing about the game

Just because I don't turn up for the match does not mean that you score points by default

The same smirk that you have on your face when you walk out of the room is the same one I have on mine as I lean in relief against the door

This girl is no player . . . I don't believe in such foolishness and immorality

But this girl, I can assure you, is a player detector

No player hater or dater!

Don't think for a second that you are going to get me to open up to you

There was a time when you would leave and then I would come after you, but now when you leave, I smile out loud cause I know you will not return, until the next time you want something from me

And I smile even more when I realize I have found the strength to not come after you!

Rich man-Poor man

The rich man allows you to sleep in his guest room

The poor man gives you his best bed

The rich man tells you to help yourself to all his expensive delicacies

The poor man spends hours preparing your favourite meal

The rich man's children say a polite hello then disappear into the comforts of their own personal space

The poor man's children form a circle of love around you and stare curiously

The rich man can afford expensive gifts

The poor man can afford to give you his best service

And the rich man,

He can afford!

René Wilmoth

Prodigal's and Prodigal's sons

Sometimes after we have wasted our living and sit in the pig pen
craving to eat what the pigs left

We feel like we have been dumped in society's most foul or gutters

We have lost our integrity, character, peace and friends

We lay there feeling depressed and lost

Below is the gutter, around is neglect and reject and above are
clouds with dark linings

We want to throw up but there is nothing left in our stomach

We want to cry but we know that will not help

We start to feel sorry for ourselves

We feel like scum from the gutters being washed down the drain
by the rain

Some of us are prodigals and some are prodigial's sons

There is a big difference between the two

Prodigals are the ones who stay in the gutter and feel sorry for themselves

The ones who spend years buried in the same spot emotionally and eventually decide to eat with the pigs because they do not see any way out

They accept defeat

Prodigals don't realize that being broken does not mean that you have been denied the right to exist,

The right to be!

It does not mean that your will or your hands are tied!

Prodigals stay forever in the 'far country' oppressed, depressed, abused and overworked

They accept a pitiful role in life as a nobody!

The prodigal's sons are the ones who have hope and confidence

The ones who discover that it is no shame to fall in the gutters, if you decide to get up and find the nearest washing station

Prodigal's sons, though they fall, never forget their identity

They do not give up their right to be, to exist, to be happy

Prodigal's sons may find themselves in strange countries but never forget their way home

They always know that it is better to serve at their father's feet than to feed pigs for strangers

Prodigal's sons always remember their father, his position and his possessions

Prodigal's sons know how to return home and ask for forgiveness!

Anatomy of a smile

A smile can light up a room

Change a heart

Break through walls

And disarm and suspend your disbelief that no one is for real

A smile is the same in any language

And when you meet people who do not speak your language

You learn to smile even more because you know they will understand

that you come in peace

So I have learnt to smile more than I did when I was young

A smile can move mountains erected to separate like us like colours from the whites at the laundry

René Wilmoth

So I have learnt to smile

It chases my pain away

I smile even when I am in pain

A smile tells a story of a dude who has been to hell and back yet makes a choice to smile

Because he can

Because in the moments when he smiles

His soul feels rested in his sweet though gentle chuckle

So I have learnt to smile

Smile like I mean it

Smile like no one is watching

Smile when no one is watching

Smile like it's my last chance to share the nurtured joy in my soul with another

And sometimes a smile breaks out into a roar of laughter as though it intends to start some kind of revolution

A breadth of fresh air

Igniting the souls of strangers as if we know each other beyond our brief encounter

Smile like it plans to set fire to our fears

Smile like it has a voice

It does

So, I have learnt to smile

There are no rules written anywhere that we can't smile when we are in pain, right?

And a frown will not take pain away

So, I have learnt to smile

I have learnt not to judge those who refuse to adorn their faces with this ornament that I wear called a smile

I have learnt not to gossip their names

I have learnt they may have grave stories to tell

Lost courage to live again

Maybe a sad smile was left somewhere on the floor of a dodgy night club or in the clutches of a broken dream

I have learnt that a smile has to have its origin in the heart

Then descend the blood vessels as though it were models strutting the runway in evening wear

Then massage the jaw bones as it steals a kiss from your lips and leaves an impression on your face

And the person on the other end of the smile will feel the realness of it

And even if they do not smile back

they will know

They will know that it came from the most intimate parts of your heart

And they may remember you for it

\

But a smile that aggressively ravishes your lips and comes only from your cheeks can be painful

You can feel the jaw bone resisting arrest as you force it from your lips

And even if the person on the other end of the smile does not know that this smile took a short cut and did not come from your soul

You own heart will know that it was cheated the right to be the origin of your every smile

And you will know and feel guilty

And wonder how you have grown so cold

So, I have learnt to smile

And smile even more

And my heart will grow to love me!

Diamond

If anybody asked me how I felt about you

I would smile, pause

Then I would tell them that you are my diamond!

The beat that my heart never thought it would need to breathe!

The brightest star on the crown that I never even cared to possess!

The oasis in my desert

The milk in my coffee

My chocolate coated dream

And if they asked me to describe your kiss

I will not know what to tell them

But I will know that it was like no other

It was ….

Different

And my heart will tell them that it was soft and wrapped in love
reminiscent of the thousand dreams that I never dreamt of you!

Then I will smile, pause

And I will think of how I never look into your eyes, for fear of starting a fire!

And I will tell them of how your smile draws me a map to your heart

And how I hope to, one day, pitch a tent in your embrace

And how you look at me as though you are ready to get me water from the moon!

I wish I could convert daylight into fireworks when I'm with you

Stop time when I'm with you!

How I want to embalm your smile

I want to be your achieved desire

Your motivation to get out of bed each day

I want to hold you like you were my first baby!

You are my first baby!

Then I will smile, pause again,

Then I will tell them

He is simply

Amazing!

Lovely me

I woke up one morning and realized that I fell in love with myself!

Don't worry, I did not break up with the man I love

I still date him on the side!

I fell in love with my ability to,

Dream

Love

Live

I see my reflection in the mirror,

My skin

Oh how I love it!

My dark skin blushes and smiles

It will not turn red

But it will glow!

How stunning

How beautiful

How sexy

How fine

'Gal how yu hot so?'

I flattered myself

I know for sure that we will be together forever!

I will never cheat on myself!

I learnt how to love myself

To think of myself

Wanting to be with myself

Loving myself

Sweet

Lovely

Me

And if you try to find me

Or if I seem a 'likkle' emotionally unavailable

I am most likely to be out on a date with myself!

Printed in the United States
By Bookmasters